Weather

Written by Sally Hewitt

W

FRANKLIN WATTS
LONDON • SYDNEY

First published in 2010 as Starting Science: Weather
by Franklin Watts. This edition 2013

338 Euston Road, London NW1 3BH

Franklin Watts Australia
Level 17/207 Kent Street, Sydney NSW 2000

Editor: Katie Dicker
Art Direction: Rahul Dhiman (Q2AMedia)
Designer: Shruti Aggarwal (Q2AMedia)
Picture researcher: Jyoti Seth (Q2AMedia)
Craft models made by: Tarang Saggar (Q2AMedia)
Photography: Divij Singh (Q2AMedia)

Picture credits:
t=top b=bottom c=centre l=left r=right

Every attempt has been made to clear copyright.
Should there be any inadvertent omission, please
apply to the publisher for rectification.

A CIP catalogue record for this book
is available from the British Library.

ISBN: 978 1 4451 1921 2

Dewey Classification: 551.6

Printed in China

Franklin Watts is a division of Hachette Children's
Books, an Hachette UK company.
www.hachette.co.uk

Cover: Angelo Cavalli/Photolibrary
Title page: Dainis Derics/Istockphoto
Insides: Inc Superstock/Photolibrary: 6t, Istockphoto:
6b, Shutterstock: 7, Maria Yfanti/Shutterstock: 9l,
Dvirus/Shutterstock: 9c, Nata-Art /Shutterstock: 9r,
Andreas Weber/Dreamstime: 10t, Alexey Stiop/
Istockphoto: 10b, Kurt De Bruyn/Shutterstock: 12t,
Arturo Limon/Istockphoto: 12b, J-C&D. Pratt/
Photolibrary: 14b, Allar Bernard/Istockphoto: 16t,
Masterfile: 16b, Caroline Penn/Photolibrary: 18,
Dainis Derics/Istockphoto: 19, Phil Degginger/Alamy:
20t, Eddie Gerald/Alamy: 20b, Garnham Photography/
Istockphoto: 22t, Mark Henley/Photolibrary: 22b,
Adisa/Shutterstock: 23tc, Roman Sigaev/Shutterstock:
23tl, Angelo Gilardelli/Shutterstock: 23tr,
Shutterstock: 23cl, Cheryl Casey/Shutterstock: 23cr,
Hasan Kursad Ergan/Istockphoto: 23bl, Ryan
Klos/Istockphoto: 23br, Christian Arnal/Photolibrary:
24t, Masterfile: 24b, William Casey/Istockphoto: 26,
CC. Lockwood/Photolibrary: 27t, Ramon Berk/
Shutterstock: 27b.

Q2AMedia Image Bank: Contents page, 11, 13,
15, 17, 19, 21, 25.
Q2AMedia Art Bank: Imprint page, 8, 14.

With thanks to our model Shruti Aggarwal.

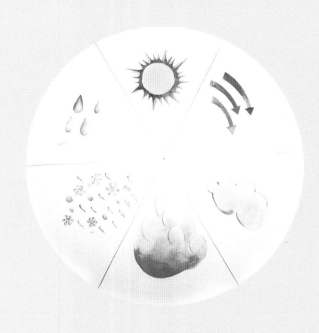

Contents

Words that appear in **bold** can be found in the glossary on pages 28–29.

What is weather?

Weather is what is happening in the air outside. Weather is how hot or cold the air feels, how much the air is moving and how much water is in the air.

When we go outside, we dress for the weather.

Why is weather important?

Weather affects us in all kinds of ways. Too much rain can bring **floods** and not enough rain can cause **droughts**. Warm, sunny days are perfect for camping, but high winds will blow away the tents! A weather **forecast** tells us what type of weather to expect.

A polar bear has thick fur to protect it from a cold climate.

Climate

Each area in the world has a particular type of weather pattern over a period of time. This is called the **climate**. Over millions of years, plants, animals and people **adapt** to survive the climate of their area.

Climate zones

The world is divided into five **climate zones**. The polar zone is always cold, snowy and icy. The cold zone has short, cool summers and long, cold winters. The temperate zone has cool winters and warm summers. In the dry zone there is hardly any rain. The days are very hot and the nights are cold. The tropical zone is hot and wet all year round.

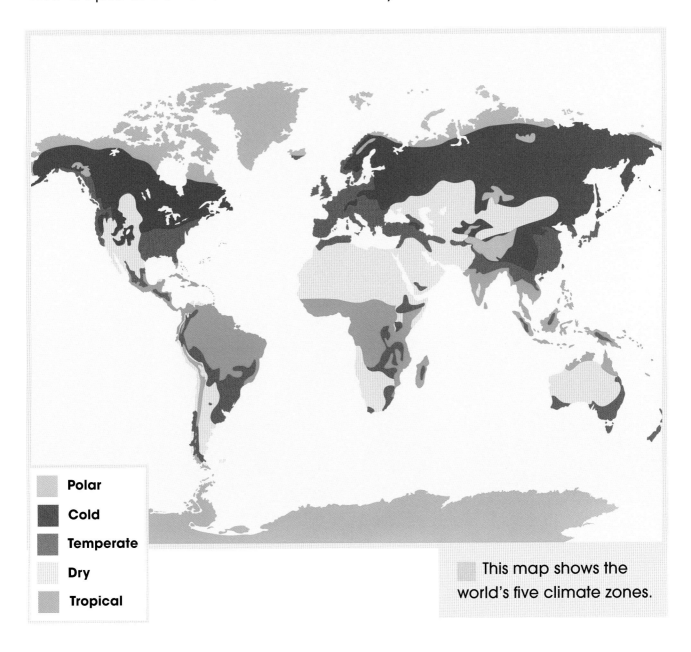

Polar

Cold

Temperate

Dry

Tropical

This map shows the world's five climate zones.

Temperature

The temperature is how hot or cold the air is outside. The Sun gives planet Earth its heat. As the Earth moves around the Sun, and clouds fill the sky, the temperature changes.

Seasons

The Earth takes a year to move around the Sun, spinning as it goes. It is tilted, so the top of the Earth points away or towards the Sun at different stages of its journey. This causes the **seasons** to change.

Changes in temperature

During the day, the Sun warms the ground which heats the air above it. At night, the ground and the air cool down. The air also cools when the Sun goes behind a cloud. We measure temperature with a **thermometer**.

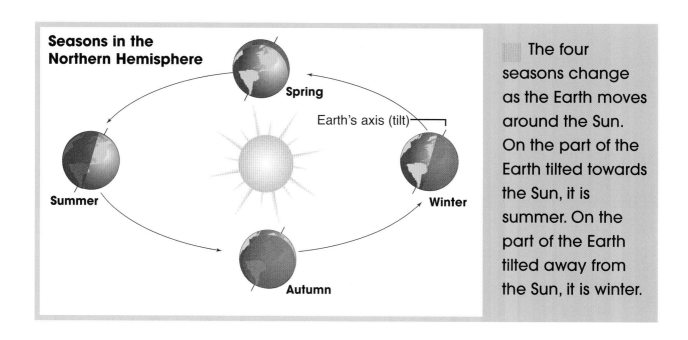

Seasons in the Northern Hemisphere

Spring

Earth's axis (tilt)

Summer

Winter

Autumn

The four seasons change as the Earth moves around the Sun. On the part of the Earth tilted towards the Sun, it is summer. On the part of the Earth tilted away from the Sun, it is winter.

Make a temperature chart

You will need:
- 2 garden thermometers (from a garden centre)
- notebook • sheet of A5 card • pencil and pens • ruler

1 Outside, hang one thermometer in a sunny place, the other nearby but in a shady place.

2 On the card, make a chart like the one below. Record the temperature in the sunny and shady places at the same time of day for a week. Mark your temperature and weather recordings on the chart.

	Mon	Tues	Weds	Thurs	Fri
Weather	☀	⛅	☁	🌧	☁
Temp 1 Sunny spot	22°C/ 71°F	18°C/ 64°F	15°C/ 59°F	16°C/ 61°F	14°C/ 57°F
Temp 2 Shady spot	18°C/ 64°F	15°C/ 59°F	14°C/ 57°F	15°C/ 59°F	13°C/ 55°F

What do you notice about the temperature changes in the different places?

Atmosphere

Our planet is surrounded by a mixture of gases, dust and **water vapour,** which makes up the **atmosphere.** The atmosphere protects the Earth from the Sun's fierce heat and stops warmth escaping into space.

Aeroplanes fly above the clouds where the air is thin and the weather is calmer. This gives a smoother ride.

Thick and thin air

The mixture of gases in the atmosphere is called air. Air is thickest and heaviest near the ground. The Sun warms this thicker air and causes it to move as wind. Air spreads out when it rises, so the air becomes thinner higher up.

Air pressure

Even though we can't feel it, air presses down on us all the time. This is called air pressure. When air falls and warms, causing high pressure, settled sunny weather is on the way. When air rises and cools, with low pressure, it may bring wet and windy weather.

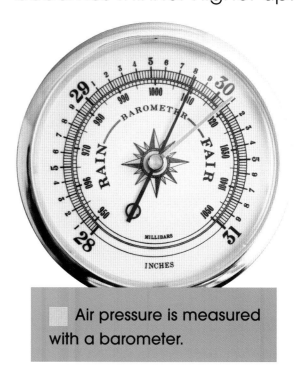

Air pressure is measured with a barometer.

Make a simple barometer

You will need:
- card • scissors • felt-tip pens
- sticky tape • straight drinking straw • large jar • balloon
- rubber band

1 Cut a strip of card about 30 cm long and 5 cm wide. Draw a Sun at the top of the card and grey clouds at the bottom.

2 Make a pointer, by cutting a small arrow shape from the card and tape it to one end of the straw.

3 Put the jar on a shelf or windowsill and balance the pointer across the top of the jar. Prop the card up so that the pointer is pointing to the middle of the card. Mark the middle with a line.

4 Cut the neck end off the balloon. Stretch the balloon over the open top of the jar so it is stretched tight and smooth. Secure the balloon with the rubber band. Make sure the jar is airtight.

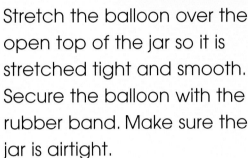

5 Tape the straw to the middle of the stretched balloon. About 3/4 of the straw should stick out.

6 Put your barometer back on the shelf with the pointer pointing at the card. High air pressure pushes down on the balloon and the pointer rises above the line. Low air pressure pushes less hard on the balloon and the pointer falls below the line.

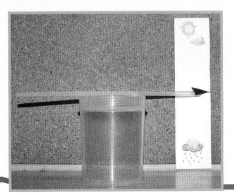

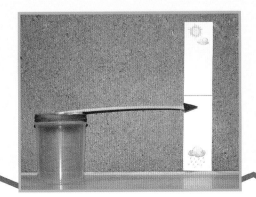

Wind

Wind is moving air. We can't see wind, but we can feel it as it blows on our skin and hair. We can also see things moving as wind blows against them.

Moving air

Changes in air pressure keep the air moving. This creates wind. Wind blows from areas of high pressure to areas of low pressure. **Global winds** sweep around the whole Earth. Global westerly winds blow the weather from west to east across North America.

Big sailing boats used the power of the wind to sail round the world.

The cups of an anemometer turn to show the speed of the wind.

Speed and direction

It can be important to know the speed and direction of the wind. High winds are dangerous for **construction** workers on tall buildings. Strong winds can blow an aeroplane off course or affect an athlete in a race. Wind speed and direction is measured by an **anemometer**.

Make a cup anemometer

Ask an adult to help you with this activity

You will need:
- 2 straight drinking straws
- sticky tape • 4 small paper cups • stapler
- drawing pin • sharp pencil with an eraser

1 Lie the drinking straws so they cross at the centre. Tape them together where they cross.

2 Place a paper cup sideways at both ends of each straw. Make sure they are all pointing in the same direction.

3 Staple the ends of the straws to the tops of the cups near to the rims.

4 Ask an adult to push a drawing pin through the centre of the straws and into the top of the pencil eraser. Hold the pencil and blow into the cups to test your anemometer spins freely.

Use the anemometer outside to test the speed and strength of the wind. The cups spin quickly in a high wind and slowly in a breeze.

Water

Water goes round and round between land, sea and sky in a circle called the **water cycle**. The water cycle keeps water on the move and changes the weather.

Water cycle

When the Sun heats water on Earth, some of the water evaporates into the air as water vapour. As it rises, it cools and turns to water drops that form clouds. The water falls back to Earth as rain, sleet, hail or snow. This is called precipitation.

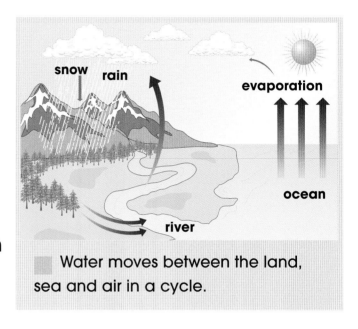

snow rain

evaporation

ocean

river

Water moves between the land, sea and air in a cycle.

Clouds can tell us what type of weather is coming.

Clouds and precipitation

Clouds form at different levels in the air. Small, white, puffy clouds come with sunny weather. High, wispy clouds tell us sunny weather will change. Towering, dark clouds bring storms and heavy rain or hail. Low layers of grey clouds bring rain, sleet or snow.

Make a water cycle circle

Ask an adult to help you with this activity

You will need:
- 2 large circles of card
- pencil • ruler • pens
- extra card • scissors
- sticky tape • paper fastener

1 Use the pencil and ruler to divide one circle into six equal segments.

2 Copy the template below to draw the stages of the water cycle in each segment. Label each segment and colour the pictures.

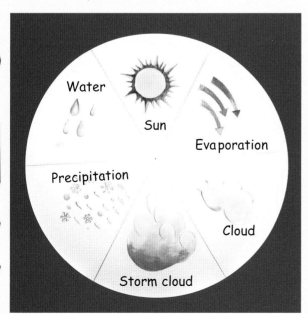

3 Take the second circle of card and ask an adult to help you cut a window the shape of a water drop. It should be big enough to reveal one segment of the first card circle. Stick a small card tab next to the window.

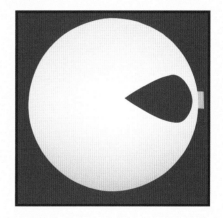

4 Ask an adult to fix the circles together at the centre with the paper fastener. Hold the tab and turn the wheel in a clockwise direction to show water going round in the water cycle.

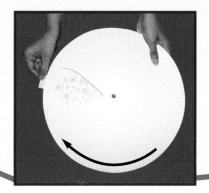

Storm!

A storm is a violent weather event. A storm can have strong winds, heavy rain and hail, blinding snow, thunder and lightning or swirling sands. Storms often cause great damage.

Thunder and lightning

When giant clouds grow like dark towers in the sky on a hot, damp day, a thunderstorm could be on its way. Lightning is caused by huge sparks of **electricity** flashing between storm clouds and the ground. It can set fire to trees.

You should stay indoors during a fierce thunderstorm, away from the lightning.

In the USA, there are about 1,000 tornadoes every year.

Hurricanes and tornadoes

Hurricanes are huge, swirling masses of wind and rain. They form over the sea and move inland where they can cause terrible damage. A **tornado** is a twisting funnel of air from a storm cloud to the ground. Tornadoes are so strong that they can pick up trucks in their path.

Tornado trick!

Ask an adult to help you with this activity

Amaze your friends by making a tornado in a bottle.

You will need:
- 2 large plastic bottles
- duct tape • sharp pencil
- jug of water

1 Take the lids off the bottles. Cover the spout of one of the bottles with duct tape. Make sure it is watertight.

2 Ask an adult to use the pencil to make a hole (a bit bigger than a hole punch) in the centre of the duct tape over the spout.

3 Fill the other bottle 3/4 full of water and turn the empty bottle upside down on top of it. Tape the two bottles together and check for leaks.

4 Turn the bottles so the bottle with water is on the top. Swirl the bottles gently and watch the water form a water tornado effect in the top bottle, with a tube of air running through the middle of it.

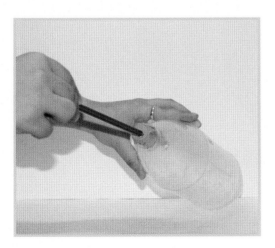

Extreme weather

When certain types of weather come together at once, they can form extreme weather conditions. Extreme weather can be very dangerous for people, animals and plants.

Floods and drought

Rain doesn't fall evenly all over the Earth. Some areas have very little rain, while others have rain most days. When there is too much rain, rivers can flood, destroying crops and making water dirty and dangerous to drink. Too little rain causes drought. Crops die and people become hungry and thirsty.

These women in Eritrea, Africa, are queuing to collect water from a well during a drought.

Extreme hot and cold

A heatwave happens when the land and air heat up and the temperature becomes unusually high. In freezing temperatures, rain can turn to hail, sleet or snow. High winds whip snow into a blizzard.

Swirling snow in a blizzard makes it difficult to see.

Make some snowflakes

Every snowflake is different but they all have six points.

You will need:
- squares of white paper (of different sizes) • pencil
- scissors • glue • large sheet of dark blue paper • glitter

1 Fold the squares in half and then in half again to make smaller squares.

2 Find the corner that is the centre of the square when it is opened out.

Turn the folded square so this corner is bottom left.

3 Copy the snowflake shape shown in the template and cut it out along the black lines. Try out some shapes of your own on the other squares.

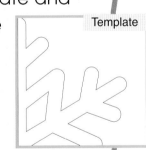
Template

4 Stick your snowflakes onto the blue card. You can add dabs of glue and sprinkle on glitter for a frosty effect.

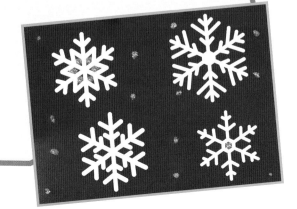

Weather forecasting

Weather forecasting gives us information about what weather we can expect. Knowing what the weather is going to be like helps us to plan a day out.

Weather check

The weather is constantly checked around the world. **Satellites** above the Earth collect information about the weather from space. This information is sent to computers to help weather forecasters work out the weather ahead.

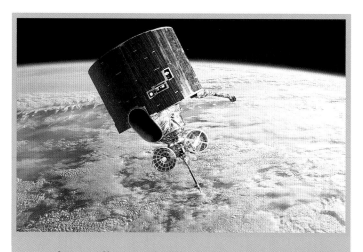

A weather satellite takes photographs and measures the temperature on Earth.

This map shows the weather forecast for North America.

Charts and symbols

Weather forecasters prepare charts with **symbols** for television, radio, newspapers and the Internet. They show us what weather to expect in the next few hours or days in a particular area. They have a difficult job because the weather is always changing.

Make your own weather station

Ask an adult to help you with this activity

Make your own weather station. Use your barometer, anemometer and thermometer, and add a rain gauge.

You will need:
- large plastic bottle
- duct tape • ruler
- waterproof pen

1 Ask an adult to cut the top third off the bottle. Turn the top of the bottle upside down. Put it into the bottom of the bottle to make a funnel. Tape around the top with duct tape.

2 Stick a strip of tape up the side of the bottle. Use the ruler and

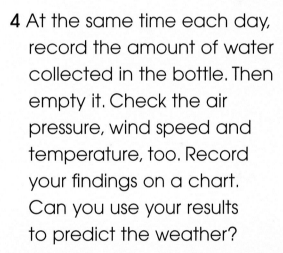

waterproof pen to write on a scale in centimetres from the bottom to the top of the tape.

3 Place your rain gauge outside in the open. You could wedge it between stones to stop it blowing away.

4 At the same time each day, record the amount of water collected in the bottle. Then empty it. Check the air pressure, wind speed and temperature, too. Record your findings on a chart. Can you use your results to predict the weather?

	Mon	Tues	Weds	Thurs	Fri
Amount of rain	1 cm	0 cm	0.5 cm	0 cm	1 cm
Air pressure	low	low	low	medium	low
Wind speed	medium	low	medium	low	medium
Temperature	16°C/ 61°F	15°C/ 59°F	16°C/ 61°F	17°C/ 63°F	16°C/ 61°F

Weather and lifestyles

The type of weather in a particular area affects the way of life of the people who live there and the type of plants that grow. People often go on holiday to experience different weather.

The Mediterranean

The weather around the Mediterranean Sea is hot and dry in summer and warm and wet in winter. People spend lots of time outdoors. The weather is just right for farmers to grow fruit, such as grapes, oranges and lemons.

Lemons grow well in the Mediterranean climate.

This shopping mall in Canada is linked to an underground train station.

Cold climate

In the cold climate of northern North America and northern Europe and Asia, the summers are short and cool, and the winters are long and cold. In some city centres, shopping malls are underground. This helps people to avoid the harsh winter weather.

Plan a day out

1 You are going on a class trip. Decide where you want to go – perhaps to the seaside or the mountains. Find your destination on a map.

2 Find a weather forecast in a newspaper, on television, on the radio or the Internet to find out what weather to expect.

www.forecast247.com

Weather Forecast

Home

Travel

Photos

Map

A warm start with a few showers. The afternoon will become brighter and mostly dry with sunny intervals.

3 How will the weather affect your plans?
   a) What will you wear?
   b) What activities will you do?
   c) What equipment will you need?
   d) How will you get there?

   How will you alter your plans if the weather changes?

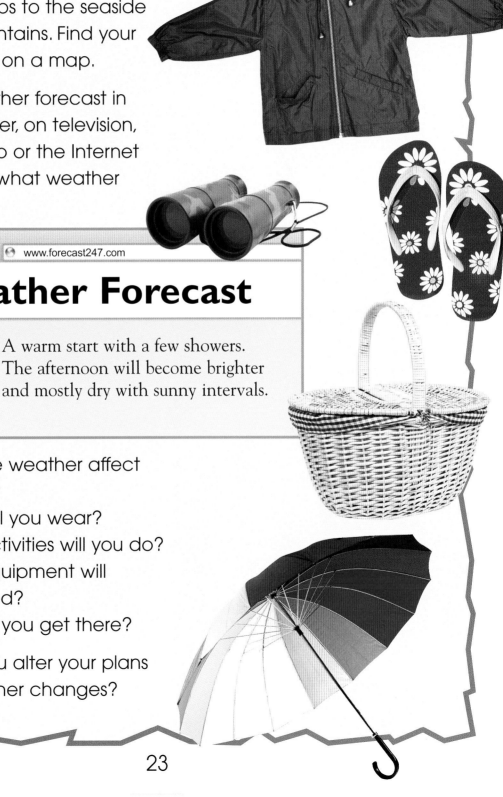

Adapting to weather

The design of the houses people live in, the clothes they wear, what they eat and drink, and the jobs they do are all affected by the local weather.

Jobs and tourism

Where there is warm sunshine, tourists come to sunbathe and swim. People work in the mornings and evenings and rest in the heat of the day. Where there is plenty of snow in winter, people enjoy sports such as skiing and sledging.

Some local people in the mountains work as ski instructors.

In Japan, paper parasols help to shade people from the hot Sun.

Houses and clothes

Where it is cold all year round, houses have sloping roofs for the snow to slide off. People keep themselves warm by wearing thick clothes. In a hot, dry climate, houses have small windows to keep out the Sun. People prefer to wear loose, light clothes.

Make a Japanese parasol

Ask an adult to help you with this activity

You will need:
- coloured pens • large and small circle of stiff coloured paper or card (20 cm across and 8 cm across) • sharp pencil • ruler • scissors
- bead • thin stick, 20 cm long
- glue • poster putty

1 Use the coloured pens to decorate the large circle. Draw a line from the side to the centre of the circle and cut along it.

2 Fold a section of the circle so it is pointed at the centre and about 1.5 cm wide at the edge. Make repeated folds back and forth all the way round the circle as if you were making a fan.

3 Stick the first and last folds together to make the shape of your parasol shade.

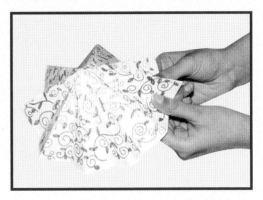

4 Ask an adult to use the pencil to make a small hole in the centre of both circles. Push the stick through the hole in the parasol shade. Glue the bead to the top of the stick.

5 Press poster putty around the stick beneath the parasol shade to hold it in place. Push the small circle up to the top of the stick to open the parasol. Pull it down to close it again.

Changing climates

The climate on our planet has been changing very gradually over millions of years. Now it is changing more quickly because of things people are doing all over the world.

Global warming

Fumes from **exhaust pipes**, factory chimneys and power stations send gases into the air. They are called **greenhouse gases** because they trap the heat of the Sun, like the glass in a greenhouse. These gases contribute towards rising temperatures on Earth. We call this **global warming**.

Global warming is causing polar ice to melt and sea levels to rise. This could flood low-lying coastal cities such as Venice.

Extreme weather

If global warming continues, we should expect more extreme weather events in the future. There will probably be less cold and frost in some places and more heatwaves and drought in others. Heavier rain will bring more floods and there may be more storms.

Climate change could mean more storms like Hurricane Katrina that flooded New Orleans, USA, in 2005.

Write a newspaper report

Research a recent extreme weather event using books or the Internet and write a short newspaper article about a similar imaginary event.

a) Describe the weather as it happened.

b) Quote an eye-witness account.

c) Describe what the place looked like after the event was over.

d) What damage was done?

e) What kind of help did the local people need?

HURRICANE HORACE HITS SMALL ISLAND

In the early hours of Monday morning, while the island slept, Hurricane Horace swept across the island tearing off roofs and ripping up trees.

Glossary

adapt
Plants, animals and people that adapt have changed over millions of years to survive in their environment.

anemometer
An anemometer is an instrument that measures the speed and direction of the wind.

atmosphere
The atmosphere is the mixture of gases, dust and water vapour that surrounds the Earth.

climate
Climate is the type of weather a place has over a long time.

climate zone
A climate zone is a large area that has a particular type of climate.

construction
Construction is the making or building of something.

drought
A drought is a long period of very dry weather when there is not enough rain for crops to grow.

electricity
Electricity is a type of energy. Lightning is a form of electricity.

exhaust pipe
An exhaust pipe is a pipe fitted to a vehicle through which fumes from burning fuel escape.

floods
Floods are caused when rivers become too full and overflow.

forecast
A forecast is a prediction of what might happen in the future, such as a change in the weather.

global warming
Global warming is the gradual increase of the world's temperature. It is partly caused by greenhouse gases in the air.

global winds

Global winds are winds that blow in one direction for long distances around the Earth.

greenhouse gas

A greenhouse gas is a type of gas that traps heat from the Sun. Carbon dioxide is one example.

hurricane

A hurricane is a very powerful tropical storm with high winds and heavy rain.

satellite

A satellite is a spacecraft that goes around and around the Earth. Weather satellites send information about the weather from space back to the Earth.

season

A season is a period of a particular type of weather. The year is divided into four seasons – spring, summer, autumn and winter.

symbol

A symbol is a simple picture that stands for something. For example, the symbol for snow is a snowflake.

thermometer

A thermometer is an instrument that measures the temperature of air or water, for example.

tornado

A tornado is a type of windstorm in the form of a funnel of air that spins over land.

water cycle

The water cycle is the movement of water round and round between air, sea and land. Rain falls to the ground and runs into rivers and the sea. Water evaporates into clouds and falls again as rain, sleet or snow.

water vapour

Water vapour is formed when liquid water turns into a gas.

Index